DEVELOPING MOBILE APPLICATIONS WITH IONIC AND REACT

IONIC AND REACT: IDEA TO APP STORE, BOOK ONE

By

MICHAEL D. CALLAGHAN

walkingriver.com

Also by Michael Callaghan

Books

Developing Progressive Web Applications with Angular (and Ionic): How to Build and Deploy Mobile Applications without Paying Apple or Google for the Privilege

Pluralsight

Over the past few years, I have authored four popular Ionic courses for Pluralsight: http://bit.ly/ps-mike

Other Courses

I have two new Ionic courses: one using Angular and one using React. You can find them here: https://bit.ly/mdc-courses

---

Note: I have hidden a discount code to my new courses somewhere in this book.

Introduction

I have been using the Ionic Framework for mobile application development since 2014, before it was even officially released. Since then, Ionic has been my go-to technology for building mobile apps. With the release of version four in 2019, Ionic grew beyond its humble origins as an angular-based framework for making mobile apps. Today, Ionic works with a variety of web technologies. It has become a first-class citizen for building all manner of web applications.

The Ionic Framework supports a variety of mobile platforms. Throughout this series, I will cover the important aspects of development with Ionic and React, going from the initial idea all the way to the Apple App and Google Play Stores.

This volume will cover the absolute basics: I will show you how to build a simple Ionic application. I will cover the application structure, explaining how an Ionic application is laid out. Next I will introduce some of Ionic's more useful UI components and create a basic side-menu for the demo application.

Unlike many books that spend a lot of time on background, this one is designed to be fast paced, with a minimum of fuss and fluff. It is all hands-on.

I expect you to have some basic understanding of web development. You should know what a <div> is, for example, and know how to create a button. You should have a decent grasp of JavaScript, but you do not need to be a master.

I do not expect you to have ever used React or the Ionic Framework, but it certainly will not hurt you if you have. I should make clear that this is not a book on React. While I will point out basic aspects of React as they pertain to Ionic, I will not go any deeper than I must to make the demo application work.

Concepts will be explained as needed, as close to their use as I can get.

By the time you complete the series, you should have the confidence you need to create and deploy your own mobile app for iOS or Android.

It will be a fast ride, so hang on.

Table of Contents

Getting Started

Prerequisites

First and foremost, you will need a decent text-editor, or integrated developer environment. I use and recommend Visual Studio Code. VS Code is a free and open-source cross-platform development environment for Microsoft, designed from the ground-up to work with all the technologies you'll be using. Of course, you're free to use whatever tool you're comfortable with.

Software Tools

Developing and deploying an Ionic application require some initial configuration. You will need the following tools, in addition to the code editor:

- Node
- NPM
- Git
- The Ionic CLI itself, installed globally

Most of the tools you will use rely on Node, a JavaScript-based runtime environment. I recommend the LTS, or long-term-support version.

NPM is a package manager built on top of node. Most of the tools you need are distributed as npm packages. It is installed with node.

Most of the tutorials for Ionic expect you to have Git, a powerful and flexible source control system, and its related tools. If you have a Mac or Linux, you probably already have it.

Quite frankly, that is about it. Installing these items depends on your platform.

If you need detailed instructions on how to do that, refer to the Appendix – Installing the Tools.

Demo Code

The demo code accompanying this book is available on GitHub, tagged for each book. Find this book's code at https://github.com/walkingriver/at10dance-react/tree/volume1-demo.

Gentle Introduction to TSX

I want to talk about TSX for a moment. React components are written in TSX, or at least the Ionic-React components. TSX is like JSX, but with TypeScript. If you have never seen JSX or TSX, it takes some getting used to. JSX is an extension to JavaScript that allows you to put HTML markup directly inside your code. TSX is the same concept extended to TypeScript. Consider this code snippet:

```
const fruit = [
  'Apples',
  'Oranges',
  'Grapes',
  'Peaches'];

return (
  <div>
    <h1>Hello, Ionic</h1>
    <p>Welcome to our app!</p>
    <h2>Here are some fruits</h2>
    <ul>
      {fruit.map((f) => <li>{f}</li>)}
    </ul>
  </div>
);
```

It starts with an array of fruits, which should appear normal to anyone familiar with JavaScript. But then, it immediately returns HTML. There is a <div> with an <h1>, a paragraph, an <h2>, and an unordered list.

Inside that unordered list is where things get a little more interesting. There is a reference to the fruit array, and it is calling a map function. The map function accepts an arrow function as its parameter, which in turn accepts each element as it iterates over the array.

Here, the array element is assigned the letter f. Each element of the fruit array gets mapped to an <li>, with the fruit of each element of the array.

Notice the curly braces surrounding the call to fruit.map. That is a sign to TSX that you are going to run some code here. Think of it as a replacement function.

At this point inside the <ul>, this block is going to get replaced with the execution of what is inside. The same thing happens inside of the <li>. Rather than display a constant value, it will evaluate the value of f, and replace the curly-brace expression with the value of f. This will become much clearer as you go.

In the next chapter, you will generate an Ionic app and see of this real code in action.

Your First Ionic App

One of the things I like to do in my home directory is I have a folder called "git". You can all it anything you want; "projects", "myprojects", "ionic", it doesn't really matter.

One thing I always do before starting an Ionic project is to ensure that I have the latest tooling, even if I installed it yesterday. I recommend you do the same. Inside a command terminal of your choice, enter the following command:

```
npm install -g @ionic/cli@latest
```

Not surprisingly, this will ensure that you get the absolute latest version there is for us.

Through the rest of this book, I am going to stick to the command line, but Ionic has a web-based tool for building Ionic projects rapidly, called the Ionic App Wizard.

Try that right now and see what kind of project it provides. Open a browser to https://ionicframework.com/start. Supply a name, pick a color, and select the side-menu template. It appears to default to React.

On the next screen, sign in or create an account. Or you can choose to skip that and just get your results.

The wizard gives you a custom-install command for the Ionic CLI, and it warns you that you must have Ionic CLI 6.3 or above, which should not be an issue, but is why I always recommend having the latest version of the tooling.

Back in your terminal, run the command that the Ionic App Wizard gave you and wait. It will run an npm install, and then you will need to cd into that directory.

Enter the following command to launch the app.

```
ionic serve
```

It should automatically open in your default browser. The application it creates looks like an email box. And voila! You just created an app out of nothing. In the next chapter, I will review the code it generated.

Guided Tour of the Ionic-React Code

index.tsx

Let us start the tour by opening the file index.txs. This the logical "top" of the application.

```
import React from 'react';
import ReactDOM from 'react-dom';
import App from './App';
import * as serviceWorker from './serviceWorker';

ReactDOM.render(<App />, document.getElementById('root'));
```

At the top of the file, you can see an import statement for the react and react-dom libraries. Every app needs to import the React namespace in order to use React. The ReactDOM namespace provides methods specific to the HTML document object model that should be called from the top-most level of the application. The App import is pulling in the definition of the application itself.

Calling ReactDOM.render() says to execute the App Component and place it inside the container specified by the second parameter. That container is an HTML element whose id attribute is root, which is in the index.html file, found in the public folder.

Index.html

Here is the complete index.html file.

```
<!DOCTYPE html>
<html lang="en">

<head>
  <meta charset="utf-8" />
  <title>Ionic App</title>

  <base href="/" />
```

```
<meta name="color-scheme" content="light dark" />
<meta name="viewport"
  content="viewport-fit=cover, width=device-width,
initial-scale=1.0, minimum-scale=1.0, maximum-scale=1.0,
user-scalable=no" />
  <meta name="format-detection" content="telephone=no" />
  <meta name="msapplication-tap-highlight" content="no" />

  <link rel="manifest" href="%PUBLIC_URL%/manifest.json"
/>
  <link rel="shortcut icon" type="image/png"
href="%PUBLIC_URL%/assets/icon/favicon.png" />

  <!-- add to homescreen for ios -->
  <meta name="apple-mobile-web-app-capable" content="yes"
/>
  <meta name="apple-mobile-web-app-title" content="Ionic
App" />
  <meta name="apple-mobile-web-app-status-bar-style"
content="black" />
</head>

<body>
  <div id="root"></div>
</body>

</html>
```

There are many meta tags in the <head>, which primarily control how the application will render on mobile devices. The folks at Ionic have already done the hard part of figuring these out, and you should not need to mess with them.

The magic happens inside the body tag, which contains a single div whose id is root. That is how the index.html and index.tsx are connected.

App.tsx

The App component is defined in this file, and this is really where your application's React code starts. App is defined as a constant arrow function, of the type React.FC. What is that all about? FC is short for FunctionComponent.

This is a function that returns some HTML, and this is what you'll see. throughout most, if not all, of Ionic code. You will look through each of these functions as you come to them. Let us walk through this file to see what that means.

```
export default Home;

const App: React.FC = () => {

  const [selectedPage, setSelectedPage] = useState('');

  return (
    <IonApp>
      <IonReactRouter>
        <IonSplitPane contentId="main">
          <Menu selectedPage={selectedPage} />
          <IonRouterOutlet id="main">
            <Route path="/page/:name" render={(props) => {
              setSelectedPage(props.match.params.name);
              return <Page {...props} />;
            }} exact={true} />
            <Route path="/" exact={true} render={() =>
              <Redirect to="/page/Inbox" />} />
          </IonRouterOutlet>
        </IonSplitPane>
      </IonReactRouter>
    </IonApp>
  );
};

export default App;
```

I want to focus your attention on the code, so I have removed the imports. They are important but are not crucial to understanding what is going on in the code itself.

The first thing you see inside the Function Component is a call to the useState function. This is a hook. If you have heard of React Hooks, this is one of them.

useState enables you to add state to the otherwise stateless function components. It takes the default state as its parameter. In this case, an empty string.

It returns an array having two elements. The first element is the object holding our state. The second element of the array is a function you can use from inside the component to alter the state.

When using hooks to manage your state, it is recommended never changing the state variable directly. So, as you look through this code, you will not see any assignments to the selectedPage variable.

Next is the markup being returned. It is everything inside the return statement.

The first thing is an IonApp. IonApp is the root Ionic component that must appear on all Ionic-React pages.

Inside of that is an IonReactRouter. This is Ionic's thin wrapper around the React Router. The React Router is what lets you create multi-page applications with rich page transitions from a website with a single index.html file, also know as a "Single Page Application" (or SPA).

Inside of the IonReactRouter is an IonSplitPane component. This is the layout that provides the side-menu that collapses automatically to a "hamburger menu" on smaller screens.

Inside of the IonSplitPane is a Menu component.You can see the menu has a selectedPage attribute, which is set to the selectedPage hook variable.

As an immediate sibling to the Menu is an IonRouterOutlet. This is where your main page content appears. The Menu is on the left, and the IonRouterOutlet houses the rest of your application.

Just inside of that are defined some routes. Think of a route as a URL. Given a path, /page/:name, the :name portion will be translated into a "route variable" called "name."

The Route contains a render attribute, which itself is set to an arrow function. A render function simply defines what happen when the route is matched. Inside that function, the setSelectedPage hook function is called with the name of the that route variable, name. Finally, a Page component is rendered, and all of the route properties are passed into it using that {…props} construct, which is known as a "spread operator." That means whatever properties were passed to the route will get passed unmodified into that Page component. The attribute exact={true} means that this route will only match if the URL starts with a slash, followed by the word page, another slash, and then by one other word, which becomes the page "name."

This will make more sense as we build some routes later.

The second route is a "default" route. It simply says that if the URL matched is a single slash character, redirect the application to /page/Inbox.

Page.tsx

What exactly is a page? As you might guess, it is another component. Look at the Page.tsx file.

```tsx
const Page: React.FC<RouteComponentProps<{ name: string;
}>> = ({ match }) => {
  return (
    <IonPage>
      <IonHeader>
        <IonToolbar>
          <IonButtons slot="start">
            <IonMenuButton />
          </IonButtons>
          <IonTitle>{match.params.name}</IonTitle>
        </IonToolbar>
      </IonHeader>

      <IonContent>
        <IonHeader collapse="condense">
          <IonToolbar>
            <IonTitle
size="large">{match.params.name}</IonTitle>
          </IonToolbar>
        </IonHeader>
        <ExploreContainer name={match.params.name} />
```

```
        </IonContent>
      </IonPage>
   );
};
```

I will not go into as much detail with this one, as you can see it
looks much the same as app.tsx. It consists of a Function
Component that returns a bunch of Ionic markup. The primary
difference here is that the FunctionComponent is a generic of type
RouteComponentProps. This is what lets the Router pass those
route parameters. In this case, it is expecting that route props to
contain just a name, which it passes into the arrow function as the
value match.

Looking down a bit, almost hidden in that jungle of Ionic
components, is an ExploreContainer. Its component definition is in
src/components/ExploreContainer.tsx.

ExploreContainer.tsx

This is another custom function component, which also accepts
some RouteComponentProps. This one is much simpler, though, in
that it only has some simple HTML, with only a single variable
expansion inside that <strong> tag.

Menu.tsx

Finally, look at the definition of that menu component.

```
interface AppPage {
  url: string;
  iosIcon: string;
  mdIcon: string;
  title: string;
}
```

Near the top of the file it defines an AppPage interface, used to
hold some common properties about a page, such as its URL,
icons, and title.

Below that is an array of Pages. So now you can see where those come from.

```
const appPages: AppPage[] = [
  {
    title: 'Inbox',
    url: '/page/Inbox',
    iosIcon: mailOutline,
    mdIcon: mailSharp
  },
  {
    title: 'Outbox',
    url: '/page/Outbox',
    iosIcon: paperPlaneOutline,
    mdIcon: paperPlaneSharp
  },
  {
    title: 'Favorites',
    url: '/page/Favorites',
    iosIcon: heartOutline,
    mdIcon: heartSharp
  },
  {
    title: 'Archived',
    url: '/page/Archived',
    iosIcon: archiveOutline,
    mdIcon: archiveSharp
  },
  {
    title: 'Trash',
    url: '/page/Trash',
    iosIcon: trashOutline,
    mdIcon: trashSharp
  },
  {
    title: 'Spam',
    url: '/page/Spam',
    iosIcon: warningOutline,
    mdIcon: warningSharp
  }
];
```

Next come the labels you can see in the menu.

```
const labels = ['Family', 'Friends', 'Notes', 'Work',
'Travel', 'Reminders'];
```

And below that the markup.

```
const Menu: React.FunctionComponent<MenuProps> = ({
selectedPage }) => {

  return (
    <IonMenu contentId="main" type="overlay">
      <IonContent>
        <IonList id="inbox-list">
          <IonListHeader>Inbox</IonListHeader>
          <IonNote>hi@ionicframework.com</IonNote>
          {appPages.map((appPage, index) => {
            return (
              <IonMenuToggle key={index} autoHide={false}>
                <IonItem className={selectedPage ===
appPage.title ? 'selected' : ''} routerLink={appPage.url}
routerDirection="none" lines="none" detail={false}>
                  <IonIcon slot="start"
icon={appPage.iosIcon} />
                  <IonLabel>{appPage.title}</IonLabel>
                </IonItem>
              </IonMenuToggle>
            );
          })}
        </IonList>

        <IonList id="labels-list">
          <IonListHeader>Labels</IonListHeader>
          {labels.map((label, index) => (
            <IonItem lines="none" key={index}>
              <IonIcon slot="start" icon={bookmarkOutline}
/>
              <IonLabel>{label}</IonLabel>
            </IonItem>
          ))}
        </IonList>
      </IonContent>
    </IonMenu>
  );
};
```

The menu itself is built with an IonList, a component designed to format items in (you guessed it), a list. The IonNote provides what appears to be a header. Then you come to some interesting code. The array map function is called on the appPages array to transform it into a series of IonMenuToggle components, which is used to toggle a menu open or closed.

Inside of the IonMenuToggle is an IonItem, used to group other components together, which in this case are an IonIcon and IonLabel, both of which should be self-explanatory.

The IonItem has a routerLink attribute set to the value of the current page's URL. This tells Ionic's router to switch to that page.

Below the menu is another list, generated the same way as the menu. The difference is it uses that labels array and contains no routerLinks.

Customize the Code

Now, before we leave this hello-ionic app, let us do a couple of fun things. How do you think you might customize that page list? If you said, "modify the appPages array," give yourself a pat on the back. I noticed that there is no Sent Mail page, so let us create one quickly and see what happens.

Put it right between Outbox and Favorites. If you are running VS Code, you can highlight the Outbox object and press Shift + Option (or Alt if you are not on a Mac) and press the down arrow. This will make a copy of entire block of code.

Select the second instance of the word Outbox to Sent Items., and the URL to /page/sent. Leave the two icons alone for now. Microsoft Outlook uses that paper airplane icon for sent items. Instead, change the icon for outbox to albumsOutline for iOS and albumsOutlineSharp for the MD. Now here is where it gets fun. As soon as you save these changes, the application will be rebuilt automatically, and the browser will reload to reflect these changes.

What do you think will happen if you now click on the new Sent menu? We did not create a new page or route, so will we get a 404? Nope, the Page component will render, with its name set to the name portion of the route, which is "Sent." This is because the Page component is itself a generic object.

Not every page will be that clean, but we will make use of this pattern in later chapters of the course.

If you want to see where those icons came from visit https://ionicons.com. For more information on the components, you can click the components link right in the middle of the hello-ionic app itself.

And that wraps up this section. You should have a completely installed Ionic development environment, know how to create a new Ionic-React app, and even do some minor customizations.

So, go forth, delight in your newfound power. Play around a bit between now and the next section. When you are ready, I hope you will continue this journey with me.

A10Dance - The Demo App

The application we will be building throughout the course is called A10Dance. It is an attendance application originally designed to help Sunday School teachers keep track of the students in their classes.

Initially, the app will consist of three pages:

- A home page
- A Student Roster page
- A Student Detail page

A side menu will let users easily navigate between the home and student roster pages. We will review how the menu is built, and navigation is configured to move from page to page.

The home page is where the application will start. There is not much here but an Ion Card component. We'll go over the basics of this component to display some text information about the application.

The Roster page displays the students registered to the class and has most of the Ionic components we will use. The students are collectively displayed using an IonList, with each list item consisting of IonItems, IonButtons, IonIcons, and more. We will spend most of our time in the section covering this page, as we flesh out its functionality with action sheets, alerts, and toast notifications.

Finally, the Student detail page is where we can view and edit various details about a single student. We'll eventually use this page to discuss Ionic forms. In this chapter, all we'll do is lay out the components and bind some data to them.

At each step of the way, I will explain the components I have selected, and then provide the code that implements them.

Creating the New Project

Now that you have seen what we are going to build, let us dive right in and get the project up and running.

Before I start any new Ionic project, I want to make sure I am on the latest Ionic CLI. So, let us do that first. In the terminal of your choice, enter the command `npm install -g @ionic/cli'. If you are already on the latest version, nothing will be installed.

Next, run the command

```
ionic start
```

When asked, select React as the framework. Next, supply the name of the project. I chose "a10dance." Select the blank template for this one. We will be implementing a side menu, but I would rather have us build it from scratch. Besides, this way we will be cutting a lot less boilerplate code.

I will not be working with AppFlow, so answer no to connecting it to an Ionic account.

Once the project is created, you can open it in the IDE to have a look. There is not much there, because you used the blank template. That is OK, because we will build it up quickly.

Go back into the terminal and fire up a quick command:

```
ionic serve
```

Take a look at how it renders.

Again, there is not much content to speak of. So, let us take care of that next.

Modifying the Home Page

The first thing I want to do is flesh out the home page, as it is the app's landing page. There will not be much content – just some text inside an IonCard.

IonCard

An IonCard is a component designed to wrap basic pieces of information. By default, a card has a gray border, rounded edges, and a subtle drop shadow. As with all Ionic components, its visual style will change slightly when rendered on an Android versus an iPhone.

Cards can be as simple or as complex as you want. The card I envision for the home page will consist of an image of a classroom, followed by a card header having both a subtitle and title, and finally a brief intro paragraph inside of an IonContent tag.

Let us get that page built right now.

Here is an image I will be using on the home page. It is available from the GitHub repo at https://bit.ly/35gNSSE.

Download that image now, or choose one of your own, and drop it into a new folder, public/assets/images. Call it classroom.jpg.

Open Home.tsx and remove everything inside the IonContent tag. Change the value inside the IonTitle tag from Blank to Home.

Next, remove the ExploreContainer component import at the top of the file. While there, delete the component file itself, which is found in the src/components folder. Delete both the tsx and css files.

In the now-empty IonContent, add an IonCard component. If you are using VS Code, it should offer to import the components for you automatically. If not, you will need to make sure you do so yourself, by importing every component you use from '@ionic/react'.

Inside the IonCard, add a standard HTML <img> tag with the src attribute set to that file you just downloaded, which should be assets/images/classroom.jpg. To be a good citizen, you should also provide an alt attribute. I am using the word "Classroom".

Here is what Home component should look like at this point.

```
const Home: React.FC = () => {
  return (
    <IonPage>
      <IonHeader>
        <IonToolbar>
          <IonTitle>@10Dance Home</IonTitle>
        </IonToolbar>
      </IonHeader>
      <IonContent>
        <IonCard>
          <a href="assets/images/classroom.jpg"
alt="Classroom">
        </IonCard>
      </IonContent>
    </IonPage>
  );
};
```

Pause here, save the file, and see what it looks like. Then you can take advantage of live reloading as we finish the page.

VS Code Terminal

Now I want to show you a really cool feature of VS code, assuming you are using it. If not, enter the commands in whatever terminal you prefer. VS Code has a built-in terminal, which you can access by pressing Ctrl+`.

Inside the terminal, enter the command

```
npm start
```

You could also use `ionic serve`, but I want you to become accustomed to using npm as your script runner. It does not matter so much now, but we will eventually rely on npm to do more complex tasks for us. So, let us start now.

If all went well, you should see something like this.

Back in the code, add an IonCardHeader component. By itself, that will not do much. So, inside that, add an IonCardSubtitle with the text "Classroom Attendance Manager," and immediately after it, an IonCardTitle with the text "@10Dance." No, you do not have to spell it in the silly way I have.

Save the file and make sure it renders. If it did not, make sure the IonCardHeader wraps the subtitle and title elements, and look for unclosed tags.

After the IonCardHeader's closing tag, add an IonCardContent tag, and inside that a normal HTML paragraph tag. Put anything you want in that tag.

The component should now look like something this:

```
const Home: React.FC = () => {
  return (
    <IonPage>
      <IonHeader>
        <IonToolbar>
          <IonTitle>@10Dance Home</IonTitle>
        </IonToolbar>
      </IonHeader>
      <IonContent>
        <IonCard>
          <a href="assets/images/classroom.jpg"
alt="Classroom">
          <IonCardHeader>
            <IonCardSubtitle>Classroom Attendance
Manager</IonCardSubtitle>
            <IonCardTitle>@10Dance</IonCardTitle>
          </IonCardHeader>
          <IonCardContent>
            <p>
              @10Dance is an attendance application
originally designed to help Sunday School teachers
              keep track of the students in their classes.
      </p>
          </IonCardContent>
        </IonCard>
      </IonContent>
    </IonPage>
  );
};
```

Save the file and check the results. It should mostly resemble what I have here.

Let us do one more thing before we leave the Home page. Put in a link to the Roster page, which we will build shortly.

After the paragraph tag, add an IonRouterLink tag with two attributes: an href attribute set to "/Roster"; and a routerDirection attribute set to "forward." This will create a hyperlink inside the card that when clicked will take us to the Roster page. Inside the tag, make sure you put some text, otherwise you will not see a link.

It should now look like this:

```
<IonCardContent>
  <p>
    @10Dance is an attendance application originally
designed to help Sunday School teachers
    keep track of the students in their classes.</p>
  <IonRouterLink href="/roster" routerDirection="forward"
/>
</IonCardContent>
```

Saving the page, you can see the link rendered. However, clicking on it will take you to a blank page. We have not built the Roster page yet. We will do that shortly.

Classroom Attendance Manager

@10Dance

@10Dance is an attendance application originally designed to help Sunday School teachers keep track of the students in their classes.

Go to Roster

Custom Students Hook

Before we build the Roster page, we will need some students to display. Later we will want to tie the list into a data store of some sort, but we do not need to do that just to get some data displayed on the page. For that, I am going to use a custom react hook.

As we saw in the guided tour, a react hook is a simple JavaScript function that returns two values inside an array. Rather than drill down into how hooks work, we can simply wrap a normal one with an array of data and expose it to the rest of the application. It will make more sense as we build it.

Create a new file in src called student-hook.ts.

Inside this file we will create an enum, an interface, a constant, and a function.

The enum is a convenience that we will use to mark a student as absent or present.

```
export enum Presence {
  Absent,
  Present
}
```

Next, create a Student object as an interface. Remember, interfaces do not exist in JavaScript, and will completely vanish upon build. Their sole purpose for us is to enable parameter type checking, code completion, and intellisense inside the code editor.

```
export interface Student {
  id: string;
  firstName: string;
  lastName: string;
  birthDate?: string;
  parentName?: string;
  parentEmail?: string;
  parentPhone?: string;
  photoUrl?: string;
  status?: Presence;
```

```
}
```

Those question marks on most of the fields indicate that those fields are optional. So, to create a valid Student object, you need to provide at least an id, firstName, and lastName. At this point, I do not know everything that a Student object should have, but these fields should be enough for our purposes now.

Create an array of students that we can use in place of a database for now. I am calling it mockStudents.

```
const mockStudents: Student[] = [
    { id: '1', firstName: 'Greg', lastName: 'Marine' },
    { id: '2', firstName: 'Jonathan', lastName: 'Bennett' },
    { id: '3', firstName: 'Neil', lastName: 'Estandarte' },
    { id: '4', firstName: 'Jennifer', lastName: 'Townsend'
},
    { id: '5', firstName: 'Casey', lastName: 'McBride' },
    { id: '6', firstName: 'Diane', lastName: 'Rivera' },
    { id: '7', firstName: 'Troy', lastName: 'Gutierrez' },
    { id: '8', firstName: 'Priscilla', lastName: 'Little' },
    { id: '9', firstName: 'Bobby', lastName: 'Robbins' },
    { id: '10', firstName: 'Edmund', lastName: 'Gardner' }
]
```

Ok, now for the custom hook.

The function I am exporting will be called useStudents, because by convention, all hooks begin with the word Use. Inside the function, I am simply calling React's useState function, passing in the mockStudents array as its default value, and directly returning what useState provides.

```
export const useStudents = function() {
  const useStudentState = useState(mockStudents);
  return useStudentState;
}
```

It is deceptively simple because it does not do much. Now let us go create that Roster Page.

Adding the Roster Page

By now, you should be comfortable adding Ionic tags into a page, but we have not created a new page from scratch yet. We will tackle that now, by creating what will arguably be the most complicated page in the application.

Back in the code editor (or at the terminal - your choice), create a new file in the pages folder called Roster.tsx.

Inside this file, we'll start by creating the simplest page we could imagine.

```
import React from 'react';

const Roster: React.FC = () => {
  return (<p>Roster Page</p>)
}

export default Roster;
```

In any page you create, you first must import the React namespace from the react library. Next, you need a new functional component (React.FC for short) called Roster to represent the page.

A functional component must return some markup, so for now, we can just have it return a paragraph as a placeholder.

Then, in order for React to be able to render the page, it needs to be exported, which you can do with export default Roster.

That lines enables other modules to import the Roster component.

If you're thinking that this will enable the Roster page to render when you click the link on the home page, it will not. You need to import it into the app and provide a route.

Open App.tsx. Scroll down to the IonRouterOutlet. We saw this in our guided tour earlier. The routing in this app is a lot simpler than we saw before, and for me, simpler is better.

Add a new route by adding another Route tag after the /home route. The path should be /roster, the component should be Roster, and set exact to true. Make sure that the Roster component gets imported at the top of the file. Now anytime we request the /roster route, the Roster page will be rendered.

```
<IonRouterOutlet id="main">
  <Route path="/home" component={Home} exact={true} />
  <Route path="/roster" component={Roster} exact={true} />
  <Route exact path="/" render={() => <Redirect to="/home"
/>} />
</IonRouterOutlet>
```

Save the file and give it a try. There is not much there, but we will take care of that shortly.

Implementing a Student Roster

Back in the Roster page, we need to get a reference to the hook we just created. Just inside the Roster functional function, add a line to call it. Remember, useStudents is essentially a passthrough to React's useState function, but it wraps and hides that mock array. Our Roster page does not care where those students come from, so we will not tell it.

Now that we have some students, let us list them on the screen.

Remove that paragraph tag and add an IonPage tag. Every Ionic React page needs an IonPage tag as its root component. As always, as we enter these next few component tags on the page, you need to make sure they are being imported from @ionic/react.

Next, we will create the page header. Insert an IonHeader Tag, then an IonToolBar tag inside of that, and an IonTitle tag inside of that. Set the IonTitle to Roster.

```
const Students: React.FC = () => {
  return (
    <IonPage>
      <IonHeader>
        <IonToolbar>
          <IonTitle>Roster</IonTitle>
        </IonToolbar>
      </IonHeader>
    </IonPage>
  );
};
```

I am hoping that the IonHeader is familiar, as we have seen it on the home page, and during the guided tour.

Immediately after the IonHeader, we need an IonContent. Inside the IonContent, I will introduce a new component: The IonList.

IonList

An IonList is another container component, designed to wrap multiple types of items in a visually consistent manner. IonLists contain things called IonItems, which in turn wrap IonLabels, IonButtons, IonIcons, form input fields and so forth. We will use all of those and more during this book.

IonLists can also be used to implement item sliding, which you have probably seen before. These are options that appear only when you swipe a list item left or right, revealing a less often used, or potentially dangerous option, such as delete.

Back in the code, immediately inside the IonList, we can iterate over the students array using the array map function. We need to provide an arrow function to "map" that will describe what we want to do with each student in the array.

Think of it this way. We are displaying a list of unknown length, but each item of the array is displayed using the same template.

Inside the map's arrow function, we'll return some markup. We'll start with the IonItemSliding component.

IonItemSliding will provide us with the item swipe, or slide, option. Inside that will be an IonItem tag. This component will encapsulate the entire list item. Inside the IonItem, add an IonIcon and an IonLabel as siblings. Set the icon's slot attribute to "start", meaning that it will appear at the start of the line. Inside the IonLabel, bind some text to the student's last and first names, separated by a comma.

Next to them, create two more IonIcon tags, which we will conditionally render based on the student's status of absent or present. The first one is for present; set it to display the eye Icon. The second is to be displayed when the student is absent, so for that one, use the eyeOffOutline, which is an outline of an eye with a line through it.

The way we render the icons conditionally is to wrap the entire IonIcon tag in a JavaScript logical expression. We compare the student's status to the value of present, or absent, followed by the logical AND operator, itself followed by the IonIcon. The short-circuiting rules of JavaScript will prevent the second half of the expression from being evaluated, if the first half evaluates to false.

Note that it is entirely possible for the student's status to be set to neither value, because the status field is optional. In that case, neither icon will be rendered, which is what I want.

Here is the completed IonContent code with the list.

```
<IonContent>
  <IonList>
    {students.map((student) => {
      return (
        <IonItemSliding key={student.id}>
          <IonItem>
            <IonIcon slot="start"
icon={personOutline}></IonIcon>
            <IonLabel>{student.lastName},
{student.firstName}</IonLabel>
            {student.status === Presence.Present &&
<IonIcon slot="end" icon={eye}></IonIcon>}
            {student.status === Presence.Absent &&
<IonIcon slot="end" icon={eyeOffOutline}></IonIcon>}
            <IonButtons slot="end">
              <IonButton onClick={() =>
clickStudent(student)}>
                <IonIcon slot="icon-only"
icon={ellipsisHorizontalOutline}></IonIcon>
              </IonButton>
              <IonButton
routerLink={`/student/${student.id}`}
routerDirection="forward">
                <IonIcon slot="icon-only"
icon={chevronForwardOutline}></IonIcon>
              </IonButton>
            </IonButtons>
          </IonItem>
        </IonItemSliding>
      );
    })}
  </IonList>
</IonContent>
```

Save the file now and see how it looks. If all went well, all of our students are displayed as expected.

Let us wrap this lesson up by finishing that sliding item. Immediately before the IonItemSliding closing tag, add an IonItemOptions slide, with the side attribute set to end. This means we want the option to appear at the end of the item, meaning when we slide it toward the beginning of the item.

Inside of that tag, add a single IonItemOption tag (mind the singular/plural here. The plural tag is the outer tag). Set this one's color to "danger", which by default is a scary looking orange/red color. We will deal with the click handler later, so for now, simply set the tag's value to the word Delete. The complete code should now look like this.

```
<IonContent>
  <IonList>
    {students.map((student) => {
      return (
        <IonItemSliding key={student.id}>
          <IonItem>
            <IonIcon slot="start"
icon={personOutline}></IonIcon>
            <IonLabel>{student.lastName},
{student.firstName}</IonLabel>
            {student.status === Presence.Present &&
<IonIcon slot="end" icon={eye}></IonIcon>}
```

```
                {student.status === Presence.Absent &&
<IonIcon slot="end" icon={eyeOffOutline}></IonIcon>}
                <IonButtons slot="end">
                    <IonButton onClick={() =>
clickStudent(student)}>
                        <IonIcon slot="icon-only"
icon={ellipsisHorizontalOutline}></IonIcon>
                    </IonButton>
                    <IonButton
routerLink={`/student/${student.id}`}
routerDirection="forward">
                        <IonIcon slot="icon-only"
icon={chevronForwardOutline}></IonIcon>
                    </IonButton>
                </IonButtons>
            </IonItem>
            <IonItemOptions side="end">
                <IonItemOption
color="danger">Delete</IonItemOption>
            </IonItemOptions>
        </IonItemSliding>
    );
  })}
  </IonList>
</IonContent>
```

Save the file and refresh the page. At this point, the only interactivity is the slider itself, so click and drag an item towards the beginning of the item. You should see a Delete button. You can click it. It behaves visually as you'd expect it to, but it won't do anything....yet.

In the next chapter we will wire up some new commands to this page so that we can manage our roster of students.

Adding Functionality to the Student Roster

If you were a teacher and this were a real class of students, there are a number of things you would want to be able to do with your app. A few of those things are:

- Mark Absent or Present.
- Navigate to a detail page to see or edit information that isn't present on the list.
- Remove a student from the class, with the appropriate warnings, of course.

In this chapter, we will enhance the UI of the Roster page to do all of these things.

The first thing I want to do is add a menu to each student in the IonList. We can either create the menu first or the button to launch the menu first. Let's create the menu first. For that, we're going to use an IonActionSheet.

IonActionSheet

An action sheet is a menu that displays like a dialog. It often contains at least two, but usually more, action buttons that are contextually related in some way. In our case, the context is that of the currently selected student.

An IonActionSheet is Ionic's specific implementation, rendering an action sheet that automatically looks at home on an iPhone or Android.

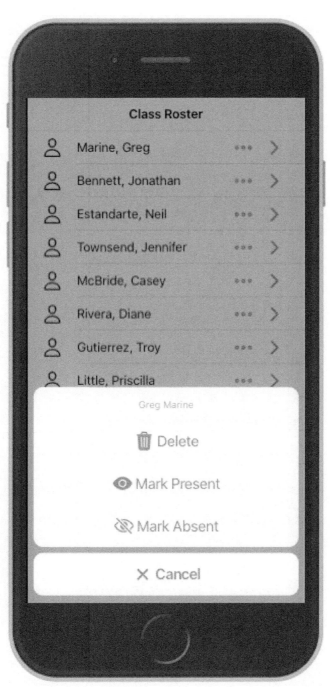

iPhone Action Sheet

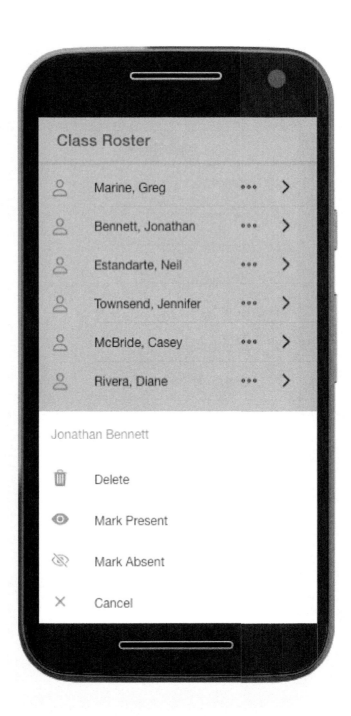

Android Action Sheet

Buttons in an action sheet may contain a "role", which can be either "destructive" or "cancel." "Destructive" is used to indicate that something permanent can happen and is often used for delete operations. On iOS devices, buttons with the destructive role are rendered differently than the rest, usually in red.

A button whose role is "cancel" will always be rendered last, at the bottom of the sheet. This button should have no other purpose than dismissing the sheet with no action taken.

The buttons in an action sheet can have text and icons. However, the way you define them is unlike a normal IonButton component.

Our action sheet will include buttons to mark a student as present or absent, delete a student, or cancel the action and do nothing. In order to do that, we need to do a bit of setup first.

In Roster.tsx, we are going to need a new hook and an object to represent an "empty student," to control how our action sheet will appear.

At the top of the file, create a new Student object named emptyStudent, but set its three required fields to empty strings.

```
const emptyStudent: Student = {
    id: '',
    firstName: '',
    lastName: ''
};
```

Then make a call to the React useState function, passing the emptyStudent object as its default. Name the return values selectedStudent and setSelectedStudent. This is a hook that will let us keep track of which student is selected, and help us show/hide the action sheet as needed.

```
const [selectedStudent, setSelectedStudent] =
useState(emptyStudent);
```

Next, create two functions to handle the click event and to delete a student from a list...

```
function deleteStudent(student: Student) {
  setStudents(students.filter(x => x.id !== student.id));
}

function clickStudent(student: Student) {
  setSelectedStudent(student);
}
```

Now it's finally time for us to add the action sheet markup.

Place an IonActionSheet tag just below the IonList's closing tag. This tag will have lots of attributes, but no child components. The first attribute to set is the isOpen. Set its value to {!!selectedStudent.id}. The double exclamation points coerce the string value into a true boolean. If the id has a value, it will be true. If not, it will be false. Because our default student in the state hook is the emptyStudent object, we can be sure of two things: Its value will never be null, and the id will either be a real value, or an empty string.

Next, create a header attribute, with its value set to the concatenation of the selected student's first and last names.

Then we want to specify the action to take when the actionsheet is dismissed. For this, we use the onDidDismiss attribute. Set this attribute to be an arrow function that simply calls the setSelectedStudent function, passing emptyStudent. That will cause the action sheet to hide itself, because the value of the isOpen attribute will become false.

Finally, we need to create the buttons array. This is an array of button objects. Each button should have a text field and an icon field, a handler function that gets called when a user clicks it, and optionally a role value. For this action sheet, I want four buttons:

1. Delete, with the role of destructive, the trash icon, and a handler function which calls deleteStudent.
2. Mark Present, with the eye icon, and a handler function which sets the selected student's status to Present.
3. Mark Absent, with the eye-off-outline icon, and a handler function which sets the selected student's status to Absent.

4. And finally, a cancel button with the close icon and the role of cancel. It does not need a handler.

Below is entire code for the action sheet

```
<IonActionSheet
  isOpen={!!selectedStudent.id}
  header={`${selectedStudent.firstName}
${selectedStudent.lastName}`}
  onDidDismiss={() => setSelectedStudent(emptyStudent)}
  buttons={[{
    text: 'Delete',
    role: 'destructive',
    icon: trash,
    handler: () => { deleteStudent(selectedStudent); }
  }, {
    text: 'Mark Present',
    icon: eye,
    handler: () => { selectedStudent.status =
Presence.Present; }
  }, {
    text: 'Mark Absent',
    icon: eyeOffOutline,
    handler: () => { selectedStudent.status =
Presence.Absent; }
  }, {
    text: 'Cancel',
    icon: 'close',
    role: 'cancel'
  }]}
/>
```

Now create a button to launch the action sheet. Open the Roster page and add an IonButtons tag immediately after the two existing icons, and right before the IonItem closing tag. Give it a slot attribute set to "end," meaning that it will appear at the end of the item. Next, add two IonButton tags, as children of the IonButtons tag. Inside of each button, add an IonIcon with a slot attribute set to "icon-only," as we do not want space in the button for a text label. Specify the icon of the first as "ellipsisHorizontalOutline" and set the second one to "chevronForwardOutline."

Add a click handler to the button with the ellipsis. When clicked, we want to call the clickStudent function, passing the current student from the array.. For now, we'll leave the button with the chevron alone for now. We'll finish that one later.

```
<IonButtons slot="end">
  <IonButton onClick={() => clickStudent(student)}>
    <IonIcon slot="icon-only"
icon={ellipsisHorizontalOutline}></IonIcon>
  </IonButton>
  <IonButton routerLink={`/student/${student.id}`}
routerDirection="forward">
    <IonIcon slot="icon-only"
icon={chevronForwardOutline}></IonIcon>
  </IonButton>
</IonButtons>
```

Save the file and have a look at the results. Click the buttons and see that they look and behave as you'd expect. The forward caret won't do anything, but the ellipsis icon should display a completely functional action sheet.

IonButtons and Icons

You may be wondering, what is an IonButtons tag, and why can we not simply drop a button where we want it? While buttons can generally be placed anywhere you want them, when used inside an IonItem or IonToolbar component, you need to group them together inside an IonButtons tag, specifying the slot as "start" or "end," depending on where you want the buttons to display. As with everything else in Ionic, "start" typically places the buttons on the left side of its parent component, and "end" places them on the right. This order is reversed for locales that traditionally read Right-to-Left.

The IonButton component itself acts as you expect and can be customized in a variety of ways. Buttons can be text-only, icon-only, or a combination of the two. Buttons can be rendered large or small, in multiple widths, and in a variety of colors. When adding an icon to a button, specify the icon's slot as "start" or "end", depending on whether you want the icon to appear before or after the button's text. To create a button without any text, specify the slot as "icon-only" and don't include any text.

The standard Ionic icons can be found at https://ionicons.com.

User Confirmation and Notification

The way the code is currently written, deleting a student from the roster might be done accidentally, if the user clicks or taps on the wrong button in the action sheet. There is no warning or confirmation requested. Likewise, when a student is deleted, there is no indication that the action occurred (other than the name disappearing from the list). We will address both of these shortcomings in this chapter.

Delete Confirmation

It is inconsiderate for an app to take a destructive action, without at least warning the user. It is better to ask the user for confirmation, and that is what we will do here. In the previous chapter, the handler for the Delete button simply calls the deleteStudent function. Instead, it would be better to get a confirmation first. We can get that confirmation using an IonAlert.

IonAlert

An IonAlert is a modal UI component that provides a simple warning to the user that something important is about to happen, and optionally provide a means to cancel it.

Below is what I have in mind to implement the confirmation. As with all Ionic components, it renders with the appropriate look and feel on both Android and iPhone.

IonAlert on Android

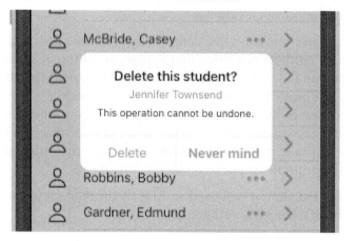

IonAlert on iPhone

Implementing an IonAlert on the Roster page will closely resemble the work done on the IonActionSheet, and with good reason. Ionic has tried to keep the component experience consistent. Much of the following code should feel familiar.

At the top of the roster page, create a new hook to control the visibility of the alert.

```
const [showDeleteAlert, setShowDeleteAlert] =
useState(false);
```

Inside of the action sheet, replace the call to deleteStudent with a call to the hook's setShowDeleteAlert, passing true. The Delete button's definition should now look like this.

```
{
  text: 'Delete',
  role: 'destructive',
  icon: trash,
  handler: () => { setShowDeleteAlert(true); }
}
```

Now when the user selects the Delete button, instead of the student being deleted immediately, the IonAlert will appear.

For the alert itself, add an IonAlert component immediately after the IonActionSheet closing tag.

There are three attributes that control the text inside an IonAlert. The header attribute is a string that appears at the top of the alert. Use something like "Delete this student?" The subHeader attribute appears just inside the alert body. Set this attribute to a concatenation of the student's first and last names, so the user knows for sure exactly which student is about to be deleted. The message attribute is the main body of the alert. Use a string such as, "This operation cannot be undone."

To display the alert, it will need an isOpen attribute set to the value of the showDeleteAlert variable.

Next, add an onDidDismiss attribute set to an arrow function to call the setShowDeleteAlert, passing the value false. This will cause the alert to disappear.

Finally, the alert needs an array of buttons. You define these buttons exactly the same way as you did for the action sheet.

The first button is the Delete button. It needs a handler that will delete a student, so provide an arrow function that simply calls the deleteStudent function from earlier.

The second button should be a Cancel button, with the role of "cancel." It does not need a handler.

A complete IonAlert implementation is here:

```
<IonAlert
  isOpen={showDeleteAlert}
  onDidDismiss={() => setShowDeleteAlert(false)}
  header="Delete this student?"
  message="This operation cannot be undone."
  subHeader={`${selectedStudent.firstName}
${selectedStudent.lastName}`}
  buttons={[
    {
      text: 'Delete',
      handler: () => { deleteStudent(selectedStudent); }
    }, {
      text: 'Never mind',
      role: 'cancel',
      handler: () => {
        console.log('Cancel clicked');
      }
    }
  ]} />
```

Save and check your work. If all went well, attempting to delete a student should not automatically work. Instead, you should now see the alert asking for confirmation. Clicking the button with the role set to "cancel" should dismiss the alert with no action taken. Only if you select the Delete button should the student disappear.

Next, we will create a small acknowledgement to the user that the student really was deleted.

Toast Notifications

Many times, an application needs to provide a notification to the user that something has happened, but it is not critical enough to interrupt the flow of the application completely. Toast notifications fill that role perfectly.

A toast is a small, unobtrusive pop-up informational banner. By convention, it should impart a short message that will appear for a brief amount of time before automatically disappearing. Some toast notifications also contain a way for the user to dismiss it early.

Deciding whether or not to use a toast notification is simple. Does the message require the user to take action? And is it important if the user misses it? If the answer to both questions is "no," then a toast notification is perfect.

IonToast

The Ionic implementation of a toast notification is the IonToast component. It is probably the most basic of all of Ionic's UI components. You can build on with a minimal amount of effort. The most basic form of the component consists of a message and a duration.

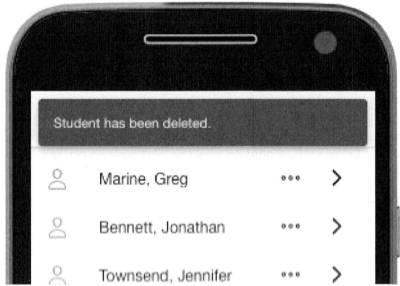

An IonToast can be vertically positioned at the top, middle, or bottom of the screen. It is always centered horizontally. It can be colored with the "color" attribute, providing any of the Ionic color constants. You can add buttons and icons. We will not be doing any of that. If you want to customize your IonToast after you finish the chapter, feel free.

Implementing the IonToast

At the top of the roster page, create another hook to use to control the visibility of the toast.

```
const [showDeleteToast, setShowDeleteToast] =
useState(false);
```

Next, modify the deleteStudent function to call the hook's set function immediate after the delete happens. My version now looks like this.

```
function deleteStudent(student: Student) {
  setStudents(students.filter(x => x.id !== student.id));
  setShowDeleteToast(true);
}
```

Add an IonToast tag immediately after the IonAlert tag. It needs an isOpen attribute set to the value of the showDeleteToast hook variable and an onDidDismiss attribute set to call the hook's set function.

Its message attribute should contain a short message indicating that the student has been deleted. Be as detailed as you want, but remember that shorter is usually better.

The duration attribute controls how long the IonToast will wait before it automatically dismisses itself. The duration is an integer and in milliseconds. Thus, be careful not to specify a duration that is too short, and definitely do not pass a string. If you omit the duration attribute, the toast will remain on the screen indefinitely, requiring user intervention to dismiss it.

The default position is vertically centered. I decided to move it to the top but will leave the final decision to you.

You can provide a buttons array to an IonToast, just as with the IonActionSheet and IonAlert. If you feel so inclined, go ahead and add one. I chose not to.

The complete implementation I used is here.

```
<IonToast
  isOpen={showDeleteToast}
  onDidDismiss={() => setShowDeleteToast(false)}
  message="Student has been deleted."
  duration={3000}
  position="top"
/>
```

Save the file and let the browser refresh.

Now when you delete a student, in addition to the student's name disappearing from the roster, you should also the confirmation toast.

If you want some ideas on how to improve this experience, I provide some in the Challenges section later in the book.

Basic Navigation Menu

Before we wrap up this volume, I want to add a menu to make it easier to navigate between the home page and the roster page. The menu will mostly look and act like the one from the guided tour from chapter one, but it will be a bit simpler. In Ionic, you create a menu with the IonMenu component.

IonMenu

The IonMenu is the Ionic component that implements a side-menu. As with most other Ionic container components, it can contain a header with a toolbar and title, along with some ion-content. The typical side-menu consists of a list of pages, made from an ion-list of ion-items.

The menu can be customized with a variety of behaviors.

If you want the menu to obscure the main page content when it opens, you can set its type attribute to "overlay." With this option, the menu slides in from the side, covering the stationary main content.

Other choices are "push," which cause the page content to slide with the menu. The menu still slides in from the side, pushing the main content out of the way.

Or you can choose "reveal" to achieve a similar, but opposite effect from "overlay." With reveal, the menu content itself is stationary, and appears to be uncovered as the main contents slides out of the way.

You can specify what side the menu is on by setting the side attribute to either start or end. If you choose end, make sure your menu icon is on the same side of the main content's toolbar, or it will look weird.

You can disable swiping the menu on mobile devices by setting swipeGesture to false.

If you want an item in your menu to close the menu when you select it, be sure to wrap it with an ion-menu-toggle component. Otherwise, the menu will stay open.

The ion-menu-toggle can also be used to open a menu (hence the name toggle). By default, it will automatically hide itself whenever it detects that its menu is disabled or being presented in a split-pane, as we will be doing here. Because of that, if you want it to be visible all the time, be sure to set its autoHide attribute to false.

Do not ask me how long it took me to debug that the first time I forgot it.

Below are examples of the three different menu types.

There is more to the menu, but those are the basics. We will build one in the next section.

IonMenu "overlay" type

IonMenu "push" Type

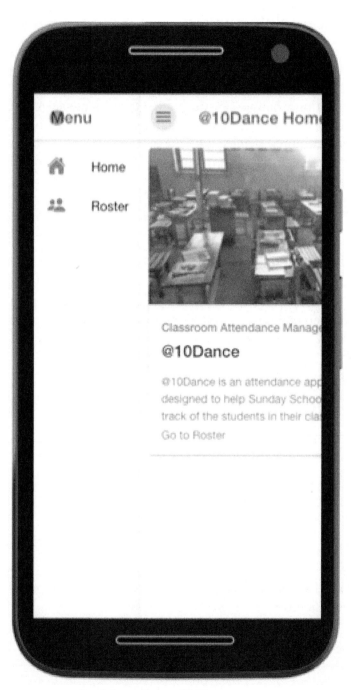

IonMenu "reveal" Type

Menu Implementation

Create a new file in the components folder. Call it Menu.tsx. This is where we will define the menu.

Replicating what we saw during the tour, create an AppPage interface near the top that will define what a page looks like. Give it three required strings: a title, a url, and an icon.

```
interface AppPage {
  title: string;
  url: string;
  icon: string;
}
```

Next, create an array of these objects. Inside the array, provide two object literals: one for the home page, with the appropriate url and icon; then one for the Roster page, with its URL /roster, and use the icon called people.

```
const appPages: AppPage[] = [
  {
    title: 'Home',
    url: '/home',
    icon: home
  },
  {
    title: 'Roster',
    url: '/roster',
    icon: people
  }
];
```

If the editor doesn't recognize the icons, you can import them from ionicon/icons.

```
import { home, people } from "ionicons/icons";
```

Next comes the menu itself. Just like the roster page, it is a React Function Component (or FC). Call it Menu and set it to an arrow function that will return some Ionic content.

To build the menu content, create an IonMenu element with its contentId set to "main." This value must match the HTML element ID of the ion-router-outlet, which is main. We will make sure of that when we add the menu to the markup.

For the type, I am partial to overlay, but feel free to try push or reveal.

Add an IonHeader, with an IonToolbar, and an IonTitle. Inside the title, provide a title such as Menu.

This is what the menu should look like at this point.

```
const Menu: React.FC = () => {
  return (
    <IonMenu contentId="main" side="start" type="overlay">
      <IonHeader>
        <IonToolbar>
          <IonTitle>Menu</IonTitle>
        </IonToolbar>
      </IonHeader>
    </IonMenu>
  );
};
```

Just after the IonHeader, add an IonContent. And just inside that an IonList. This is where the menu will be constructed, by iterating over the appPages array.

Open a curly brace to execute some code. Call the appPages array's map function. This function gets an arrow function to be executed for each element of the array. That function will receive two parameters, the page object and the array index of that object. The arrow function needs to return the markup for each object.

The first element is an IonMenuToggle with its key set to the index variable. If we don't provide this index, React will complain that each child in a list should have a key. It will still render, but it logs an ugly warning, and we do not need to see that.

As I mentioned earlier, set the autoHide property to false, unless you enjoy watching things vanish for no apparent reason.

Inside the toggle, place an IonItem with a routerLink set to appPage.url. Doing this automatically turns the item into a hyperlink, which is pretty cool. Make sure you get the binding syntax right, as I'm showing here. Otherwise, you could end up sending your users to a route literally called "appPage.url." Set the routerDirection to none or root, your choice. This affects the animation. It is subtle, so play with it and decide which you prefer.

If you want a visible line separating your menu items, set the lines attribute to "full" or omit the attribute entirely. I am not a fan of the looks, so I tend to choose "none."

Finally, set detail={false}. That will prevent the menu from having a gray forward chevron on its side. I do not like the effect for a menu.

Inside the item, add an IonIcon with its slot set to start and its icon set to the appPage.icon. Again, pay attention to the binding syntax.

Your complete menu should look like this. Make sure you close all your tags properly, and that all of your curly braces are closed.

```
const Menu: React.FC = () => {
  return (
    <IonMenu contentId="main" side="start" type="overlay">
      <IonHeader>
        <IonToolbar>
          <IonTitle>Menu</IonTitle>
        </IonToolbar>
      </IonHeader>
      <IonContent>
        <IonList>
          {appPages.map( (appPage, index) => {
            return (
              <IonMenuToggle key={index} autoHide={false}>
                <IonItem routerLink={appPage.url}
routerDirection="root" lines="none">
                  <IonIcon slot="start"
icon={appPage.icon} />
                  <IonLabel>{appPage.title}</IonLabel>
```

```
                </IonItem>
              </IonMenuToggle>
            );
          })}
        </IonList>
      </IonContent>
    </IonMenu>
  );
};
```

There is only one line left. We need to export the Menu function, otherwise we will not be able to import it into the App. Add the following line to the bottom of Menu.tsx.

```
export default Menu;
```

Add Menu to Application

To make the menu visible, open the App.tsx page.

Immediately inside the IonReactRouter as its first child, add an IonSplitPane component with its contentId set to "main." Make sure the split pane completely wraps the IonRouterOutlet.

Add the Menu tag as the first child of the IonSplitPane, immediately before the IonRouterOutlet. We already added the route to the roster page, but in case you did not, you need it here inside the IonRouterOutlet.

Finally, for this file, you need to set the IonRouterOutlet's id to "main." The complete Function Component in App.tsx should now look like this.

```
const App: React.FC = () => (
  <IonApp>
    <IonReactRouter>
      <IonSplitPane contentId="main">
        <Menu />
        <IonRouterOutlet id="main">
```

```
        <Route path="/home" component={Home}
exact={true} />
        <Route path="/roster" component={Roster}
exact={true} />
        <Route exact path="/" render={() => <Redirect
to="/home" />} />
      </IonRouterOutlet>
    </IonSplitPane>
  </IonReactRouter>
</IonApp>
);
```

Menu Button

Next, we need to add a menu icon to both of our pages. Nope, it is not automatic. Open Home.tsx.

Inside the IonToolbar, just before the IonTitle, you need to add an IonButtons component with slot="start". Then an IonMenuButton component inside of that.

You don't need to add any text or icons. Those will be managed automatically. Then you need to do exactly the same code in the Roster page. Just copy and paste the same block of code.

Both page's headers should now look like this.

```
<IonHeader>
  <IonToolbar>
    <IonButtons slot="start">
      <IonMenuButton />
    </IonButtons>
    <IonTitle>Home</IonTitle>
  </IonToolbar>
</IonHeader>
```

Save the files and give it a try.

If all went well, you should now be able to navigate between the home and roster pages with ease.

Wrap Up

To recap what just happened in this Chapter: if you want to add a page, these are the things you should do:

- Create the page component itself, with the markup and code you want.
- Add a route with a URL so that users can get to the page.
- If you want the page in your application's side menu, add it to the appPages array, with the URL, a title, and an icon.
- Repeat as needed.

There will be more pages in future volumes of this series. I hope you will join me.

Where to Go from Here?

I hope you enjoyed this introduction to developing web applications with Ionic and React. By this point, you should be comfortable with:

- The basics of the Ionic Framework.
- The peculiarity of the TSX syntax.
- Looking for more information in the Ionic Documentation.

This is Volume One in the series: *Ionic and React: Idea to App Store*. Please look for the other volumes in this series.

Ionic and React Video Course

I mentioned this before, but it bears repeating. There is also an online video version of this course, encompassing this entire book series.

As a thank-you for reading this book, I am offering a discount code, which is the string I used for the icon indicating that a student has been marked absent on the Roster page.

Simply enroll for either of my Ionic courses at https://bit.ly/mdc-courses, and enter the discount code. Case should not matter, but if it does, please enter the code in UPPERCASE.

Apply What You Have Learned

Now that you have completed this volume, take a few moments to apply what you have learned to the demo application you just built. Here are a few enhancements you attempt.

Modify the "Delete" Toast

The toast notification we added to indicate that a student was deleted from the roster positions itself at the top of the screen, stays for 3000 ms (3 seconds), and then vanishes. It cannot be manually dismissed by the user. And sometimes, it can be a little hard to see in its default color and position. Your challenge is to fix that.

1. Change the duration of the toast to 5 seconds.
2. Add a close button so the user can close the toast sooner. Toast buttons are configured the same way that Action Sheet buttons are. Hint: use a role rather than a handler.
3. Move the toast to the bottom or middle of the screen using its position attribute.
4. Change its color.

Modify the Icons

Maybe you do not like my icons. Head over to https://ionicons.com and find some you like better. Here are some ideas:

1. You can change the absent/present icons to something else, change their colors, or both.
2. The icon we use in the roster is pretty generic. You could add a gender to the Student interface and then adjust the icon based on that value at runtime.
3. Change the color of any icon.

Advanced: Undo Delete

Instead of a close button on the toast notification, you could add a quick "undo" button.

Advanced: Sort Roster

TypeScript arrays have a sort function. Provide a button in the Roster toolbar to sort by the students' last names instead of the current default.

Advanced: Header Component

It seems that every page needs a header with a title and menu button. For a demo application with only two pages, copying and pasting the header code might be acceptable. As your app grows, this might become a burden. Create a custom component that includes a menu button, with a title you can pass as an attribute.

References

https://ionicframework.com/docs

Appendix – Installing the Tools

Windows Quick Start

If you are on Windows, this section should get you up and running as quickly as possible. I am going to assume you do not have any of the following tools. If you do, please just skip that step.

Git

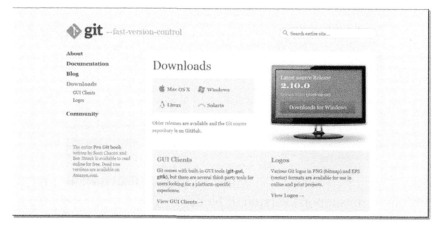

First, you will need the latest version of Git. Depending on your code editor or IDE of choice, it is possible to avoid typing most git commands.

Git for Windows installs an alternative command prompt, called Git Bash. I recommend using that over the windows command prompt wherever possible.

You should be able to click the Downloads for Windows button, select the default for your system (probably the 64-bit Git for Windows, and then install with the default options.

Node

Next, you will need to have NodeJS, which will become the foundation of everything you do in this book.

The most straightforward method is downloading and installing it right from nodejs.org. It is quick and painless. The only real drawback is that it limits you to only one version of Node being installed at a time. Believe it or not, that can be a real problem for some developers, who support multiple apps, each built on a different version of Node. It will not be a problem for this book, so you are safe in installing from here.

Visit https://nodejs.org. You will want to download the latest LTS (or long-term support) version of Node.

Once downloaded, simply run the installer. Accepting the installer's defaults should get you what you need.

macOS Quick Start

If you use a Mac, this section will show you how to install the tools you are going to need. If you are not using a Mac, feel free to skip ahead to the next section.

Homebrew

On a Mac, most of the tools you need to install can be installed through Homebrew. Homebrew bills itself as the Mac's missing package manager.

There are a lot of tools and runtime packages available through Homebrew, so I recommend installing it if you do not already have it. You can install it by copying and pasting the following command into any terminal window.

```
/bin/bash -c "$(curl -fsSL
https://raw.githubusercontent.com/Homebrew/install/master/
install.sh)"
```

Git

Next you should install Git. But first, check to see if you have it. In a terminal window, enter the command

```
git --version
```

If it is installed, you will see a version number, probably 2.x or something. If you have a version that says, "Apple Git", it means you installed it through the XCode command line tools. This should be ok.

If you do not have git, and you installed Homebrew, simply issue the command

---

```
brew install git
```

This will give you the latest version for your system.

If you prefer to install git from the official site, you can do that, too. Head over to https://git-scm.com, click the download button, and follow the instructions.

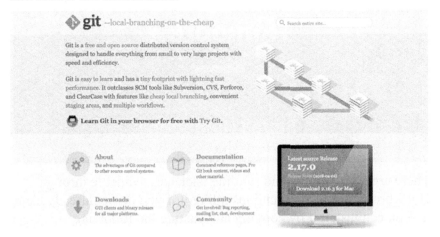

Node

Next, tackle node. There are three ways to install node. Each is valid and has its own positives and negatives. I will try to give you enough information for you to make an intelligent choice. Review them and choose the one you prefer.

If you like installing items from their source, feel free to head over to https://nodejs.org and click the big green button. The tools you are going to be using require at least Node 8, so you should not have any issues here. I recommend downloading and installing the LTS, or long-term-support version.

Node.js® is a JavaScript runtime built on Chrome's V8 JavaScript engine.

Download for macOS (x64)

12.16.2 LTS	13.13.0 Current
Recommended For Most Users	Latest Features

Other Downloads | Changelog | API Docs   Other Downloads | Changelog | API Docs

Or have a look at the Long Term Support (LTS) schedule.

Sign up for Node.js Everywhere, the official Node.js Monthly Newsletter.

Node (Homebrew)

You can also use Homebrew to install node. Simply enter the
following command in a terminal window.

```
brew install node
```

While it is installing, I would like to point out a few things that you
will be seeing. The first thing Homebrew tries to do is update its
local indexes. This is how it knows what software is available. The
massive amount of text that fills the screen are all the new or
updated software packages that Homebrew has been found since
the last time it was run on this system.

Homebrew then finds node and its dependencies. It continues to
download and install the dependencies, and finally, it installs node
itself.

After not too long, depending on your internet connection, node is
installed.

Note that the version of Node that gets installed should be the
latest version available. You could have changed the brew
command to specify a different version. And you are still stuck
with just a single version of node, which may or may not be what
you need all the time.

Fortunately, there is a better way, which I describe in detail later.

Linux Quick Start

If you plan to follow along on Linux, the tools should be straightforward

These steps were tested on Ubuntu Desktop 18.10, Cosmic Cuttlefish, which uses Debian packages. If you use a different version of Linux, you will need to alter these steps to work with your distribution's package manager.

There are two things you need to install: Node and Git.

There are three ways to install node. Each is valid and has its own its own positives and negatives. I will try to give you enough information for you to make an intelligent choice. Review them and choose the one you prefer.

The first method is to download directly from nodejs.org itself. Quite frankly, I do not recommend this method. However, if you like installing items from their official locations, feel free to head over to https://nodejs.org and click the big green button. I recommend downloading and installing the LTS, or long-term-support version.

Another way is to install node from the Ubuntu command line. Open a terminal window and type

```
node --version
```

to see if you already have it. In my pristine system, I do not. But Ubuntu tells me exactly how to get it.

To install it, simply enter the command provided, which should be

```
sudo apt-get install node
```

and it gets installed.

Now when you type node --version, you should see that the default Ubuntu version was installed. In my case, I got 8.10. So that is the second way, and it is better than the first, though you probably are not getting the LTS version. Fortunately, there is a third method, which is far more flexible. I describe that in the next section.

Node Version Manager

Now let us review another way to install Node on macOS and Linux. My preferred approach to anything relating to node and npm is to install a tool called the Node Version Manager, or nvm. It is a little more involved, but far more flexible in the long run.

What is nvm? It is an elegant set of shell script functions to enable the most flexible use of node imaginable.

The primary purpose of nvm is to enable you to install and switch between multiple versions of node and npm instantly. So, if you happen to have one project that requires Node 8, but another one that requires Node 4, for example, it is easy to keep them both installed, yet still independent from one another.

To me, the more important features of nvm revolve around root, or administrator access. Many npm package installation instructions you will find on the web instruct you to use the sudo (or super-user do) command to install packages globally. It is possible that you may not have root access to your Mac, making those instructions worthless. There are workarounds, naturally, and they work fine. I used such workarounds for a few years before a colleague showed me nvm. Now I am convinced.

Once you commit to nvm, there is no reason ever to use sudo. In fact, you do not even need root access to install nvm. Everything gets installed under your own user account.

On macOS, install nvm with this command. It uses Homebrew, which you should now have.

```
brew install nvm
```

If you are on Linux, use this command, as these tools should exist on a stock Linux system.

```
wget -qO- https://raw.githubusercontent.com/nvm-sh/nvm/v0.35.3/install.sh | bash
```

One you have installed nvm, you can use it to install any version of node that you want. In this case, you will install the latest stable version. Simply execute the commands shown here.

Command	Description
nvm install 'lts/*'	Download and install the latest long-term-support, or LTS, version of Node.
node --version nvm current	Determine which version of node is currently in use.
nvm ls	Determine which versions of node you have installed
nvm ls-remote	Determine what versions of node are available to you. Warning: It is a pretty long list.
nvm install v10.15	Install any available version of node (the v is optional).
nvm use v12.4	Switch to another version of nvm you have installed (the v is optional)

From this point forward, all of node and every npm package you install globally will be placed in the .nvm directory inside of your home directory. You should never have to use sudo to install an npm package globally. You're welcome.

Install Ionic

Finally, you need to install Ionic. Fortunately, this step is identical no matter which OS you use. Simply open the terminal of your choice and enter the following command

```
npm install -g @ionic/cli
```

This command will download and install the Ionic Framework tooling globally (that's what the -g flag does). Once installed, this tooling, known as the Ionic CLI, provides a variety of commands to help you in your Ionic development. Some of the important commands are shown here.

Command	Description
ionic info	Prints project, system, and environment information.
ionic docs	Opens the Ionic documentation website.
ionic start	Creates a new project
ionic generate	Creates new project assets (pages, components, interfaces, services, etc.). Note, this command currently only supports Ionic-Angular projects.

Printed in Great Britain
by Amazon

40402808R00047